ADAM

BY BRIAN BASSET

Foreword by Jeff Smith

Andrews and McMeel   A Universal Press Syndicate Company   **Kansas City · New York**

ISBN: 0-8362-1841-8

Library of Congress Catalog Card Number: 88-83869

FOR LINDA

FOREWORD

Adam cracks me up! He lives on the brink of the schizophrenia that most men know. He is a househusband, but he wants to be a part-time stud and jock . . . and he doesn't even have much time to fantasize. He looks for respect and receives none . . . not even for his tuna casserole or for the pain involved in learning that housework is just that . . . a pain. Will his children grow up with a confused image of what a father really should be? No, they will actually come to see men in a much more realistic way, and in turn both the children and Adam will be set free from the boring stereotype that plagues so many men in our culture.

Prophets are not to tell the future. They are to tell the truth. Brian Basset is a prophet in that sense. He puts Adam, the first man, the New-man, right out in front of all of us, and delights us since we are just as bewildered as Adam. The hilarious truths that come from Basset's insights are healing, and that is why I continue to look for his strip first. But, green jelly beans in a meatball Stroganoff as a symbol of a bit more creativity in the kitchen? Come on Adam, this is sick!

—JEFF SMITH
The Frugal Gourmet

5

7

11

15

24

29

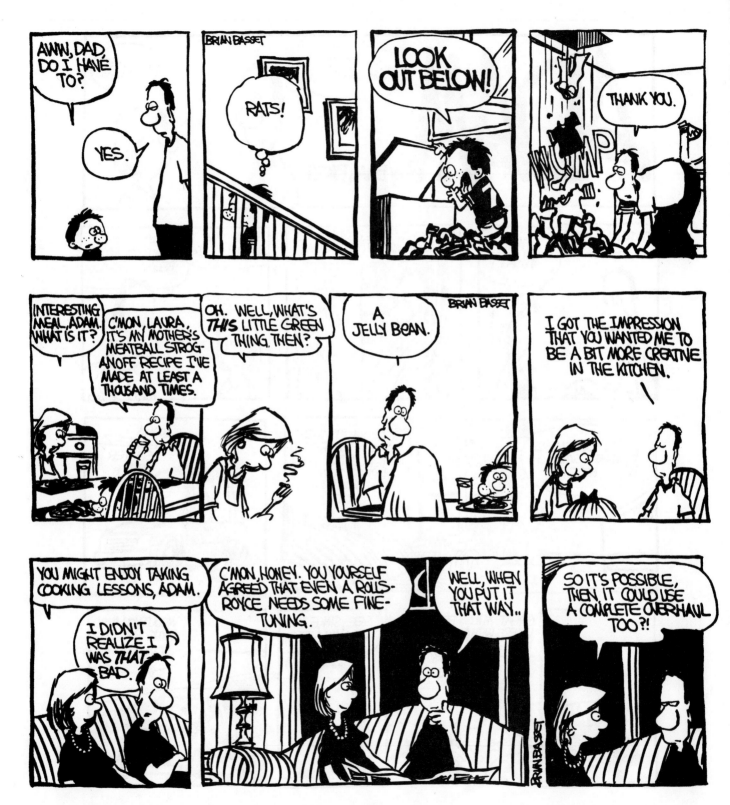

31

41

43

44

48

49

56

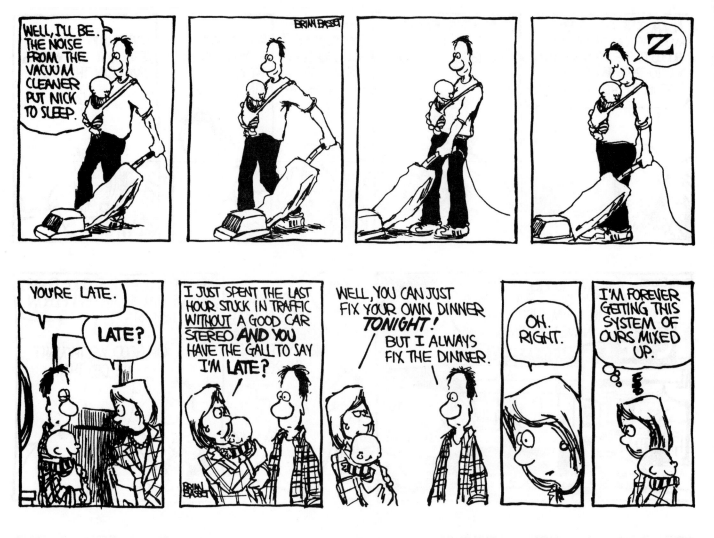

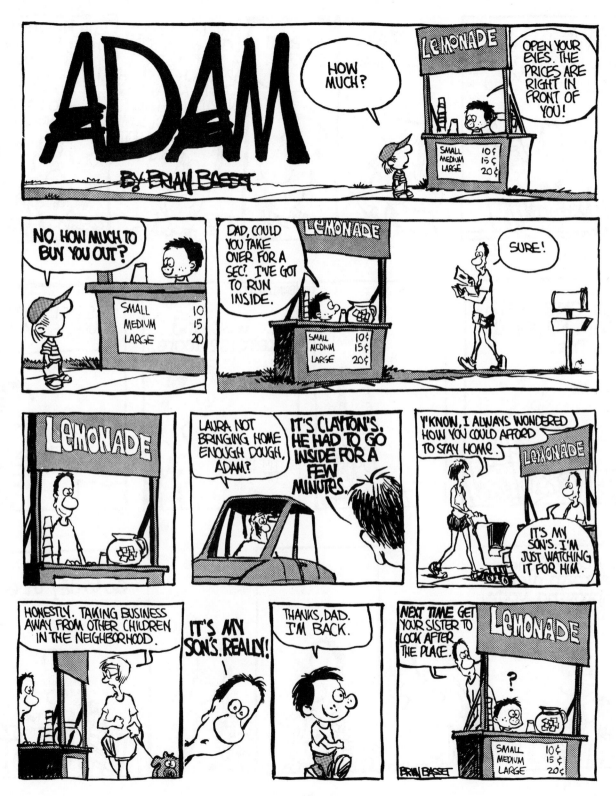

65

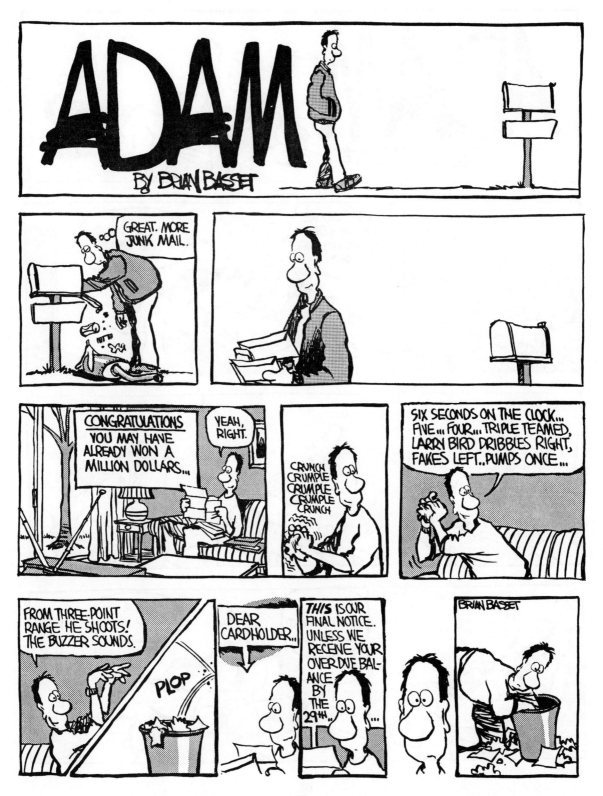

75

92

100

110

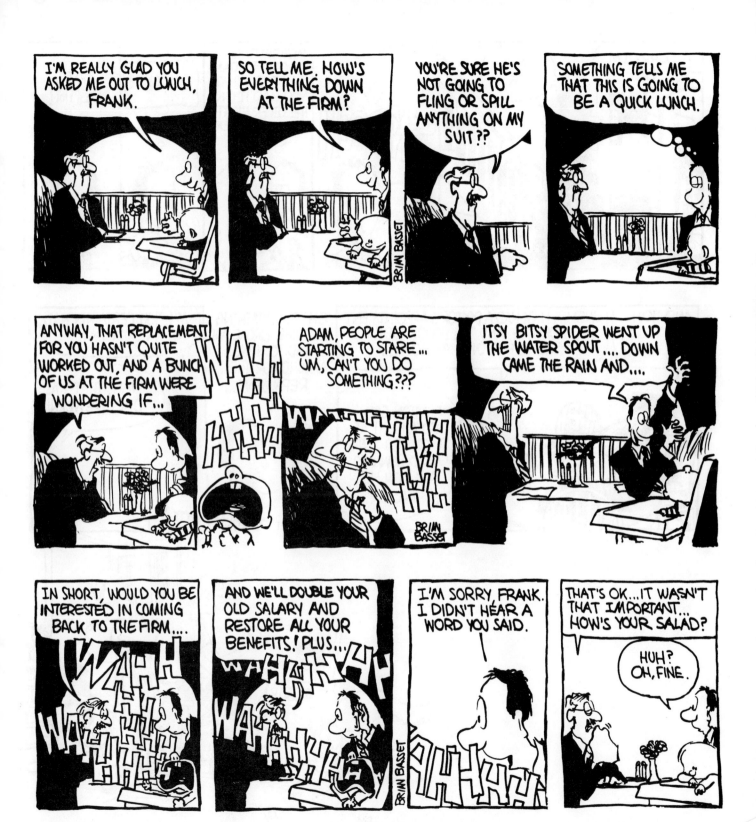

MOUNTAIN SUN PRODUCTIONS
P. O. BOX 11331
SANTA ANA, CA 92711-1331

THE END